You yourself, as much as anybody in the entire universe,

deserve your love and affection.

Buddha

This journal belongs to:

My Self-Care Vision Statement

Date: _____ / _____ / _____

_Considering my goal and what I would like my self-care to look like in the long term, this is my vision statement...

My Self-Care Goals

Date: _____ / _____ / _____

30 Day Self-Care Goals

....
....
....
....
....
....
....

10 Day Self-Care Goals

....
....
....
....
....
....
....

Long Term Self-Care Goals

....
....
....
....
....
....
....

What I'm working at now to achieve these goals?

....
....
....
....
....
....
....

Special Notes

My Self-Care Vision Statement

Date: _____ / _____ / _____

_Considering my goal and what I would like my self-care to look like in the long term, this is my vision statement…

My Self-Care Goals

Date: _____ / _____ / _____

30 Day Self-Care Goals

10 Day Self-Care Goals

Long Term Self-Care Goals

What I'm working at now to achieve these goals?

Special Notes

My Self-Care Vision Statement

Date: _____ / _____ / _____

Considering my goal and what I would like my self-care to look like in the long term, this is my vision statement...

My Self-Care Goals

Date: _____ / _____ / _____

30 Day Self-Care Goals

....
....
....
....
....
....
....

10 Day Self-Care Goals

....
....
....
....
....
....
....

Long Term Self-Care Goals

....
....
....
....
....
....
....

What I'm working at now to achieve these goals?

....
....
....
....
....
....
....

Special Notes

My Self-Care Vision Statement

Date: _____ / _____ / _____

_Considering my goal and what I would like my self-care to look like in the long term, this is my vision statement...

My Self-Care Goals

Date: _____ / _____ / _____

30 Day Self-Care Goals

....
....
....
....
....
....
....
....

10 Day Self-Care Goals

....
....
....
....
....
....
....
....

Long Term Self-Care Goals

....
....
....
....
....
....
....

What I'm working at now to achieve these goals?

....
....
....
....
....
....
....

Special Notes

My Self-Care Vision Statement

Date: _____ / _____ / _____

Considering my goal and what I would like my self-care to look like in the long term, this is my vision statement...

My Self-Care Goals

Date: ____ / ____ / ____

30 Day Self-Care Goals

....
....
....
....
....
....
....

10 Day Self-Care Goals

....
....
....
....
....
....
....

Long Term Self-Care Goals

....
....
....
....
....
....
....

What I'm working at now to achieve these goals?

....
....
....
....
....
....
....

Special Notes

My Self-Care Vision Statement

Date: _____ / _____ / _____

Considering my goal and what I would like my self-care to look like in the long term, this is my vision statement...

My Self-Care Goals

Date: _____ / _____ / _____

30 Day Self-Care Goals

....
....
....
....
....
....
....
....

10 Day Self-Care Goals

....
....
....
....
....
....
....
....

Long Term Self-Care Goals

....
....
....
....
....
....
....
....

What I'm working at now to achieve these goals?

....
....
....
....
....
....
....
....

Special Notes

My Self-Care Vision Statement

Date: _____ / _____ / _____

Considering my goal and what I would like my self-care to look like in the long term, this is my vision statement...

My Self-Care Goals

Date: _____ / _____ / _____

30 Day Self-Care Goals

....
....
....
....
....
....

10 Day Self-Care Goals

....
....
....
....
....
....

Long Term Self-Care Goals

....
....
....
....
....
....

What I'm working at now to achieve these goals?

....
....
....
....
....
....
....

Special Notes

My Self-Care Vision Statement

Date: _____ / _____ / _____

_Considering my goal and what I would like my self-care to look like in the long term, this is my vision statement...

My Self-Care Goals

Date: _____ / _____ / _____

30 Day Self-Care Goals

....
....
....
....
....
....
....

10 Day Self-Care Goals

....
....
....
....
....
....
....

Long Term Self-Care Goals

....
....
....
....
....
....
....

What I'm working at now to achieve these goals?

....
....
....
....
....
....
....

Special Notes

My Self-Care Vision Statement

Date: _____ / _____ / _____

Considering my goal and what I would like my self-care to look like in the long term this is my vision statement...

My Self-Care Goals

Date: _____ / _____ / _____

30 Day Self-Care Goals

....
....
....
....
....
....
....

10 Day Self-Care Goals

....
....
....
....
....
....
....

Long Term Self-Care Goals

....
....
....
....
....
....
....

What I'm working at now to achieve these goals?

....
....
....
....
....
....
....

Special Notes

My Self-Care Vision Statement

Date: _____ / _____ / _____

Considering my goal and what I would like my self-care to look like in the long term, this is my vision statement...

My Self-Care Goals

Date: _____ / _____ / _____

30 Day Self-Care Goals

....
....
....
....
....
....
....

10 Day Self-Care Goals

....
....
....
....
....
....
....

Long Term Self-Care Goals

....
....
....
....
....
....
....

What I'm working at now to achieve these goals?

....
....
....
....
....
....
....

Special Notes

My Self-Care Vision Statement

Date: _____ / _____ / _____

Considering my goal and what I would like my self-care to look like in the long term, this is my vision statement...

My Self-Care Goals

Date: ____ / ____ / ____

30 Day Self-Care Goals

....
....
....
....
....
....
....

10 Day Self-Care Goals

....
....
....
....
....
....
....

Long Term Self-Care Goals

....
....
....
....
....
....
....

What I'm working at now to achieve these goals?

....
....
....
....
....
....
....

Special Notes

My Self-Care Vision Statement

Date: _____ / _____ / _____

Considering my goal and what I would like my self-care to look like in the long term, this is my vision statement...

My Self-Care Goals

Date: _____ / _____ / _____

30 Day Self-Care Goals

10 Day Self-Care Goals

Long Term Self-Care Goals

What I'm working at now to achieve these goals?

Special Notes

My Self-Care Vision Statement

Date: _____ / _____ / _____

_Considering my goal and what I would like my self-care to look like in the long term, this is my vision statement...

My Self-Care Goals

Date: _____ / _____ / _____

30 Day Self-Care Goals

....
....
....
....
....
....
....

10 Day Self-Care Goals

....
....
....
....
....
....
....

Long Term Self-Care Goals

....
....
....
....
....
....
....
....

What I'm working at now to achieve these goals?

....
....
....
....
....
....
....
....

Special Notes

My Self-Care Vision Statement

Date: _____ / _____ / _____

_Considering my goal and what I would like my self-care to look like in the long term, this is my vision statement...

My Self-Care Goals

Date: _____ / _____ / _____

30 Day Self-Care Goals

....
....
....
....
....
....
....

10 Day Self-Care Goals

....
....
....
....
....
....
....

Long Term Self-Care Goals

....
....
....
....
....
....
....
....

What I'm working at now to achieve these goals?

....
....
....
....
....
....
....
....

Special Notes

My Self-Care Vision Statement

Date: _____ / _____ / _____

_Considering my goal and what I would like my self-care to look like in the long term, this is my vision statement...

My Self-Care Goals

Date: _____ / _____ / _____

30 Day Self-Care Goals

....
....
....
....
....
....
....

10 Day Self-Care Goals

....
....
....
....
....
....
....

Long Term Self-Care Goals

....
....
....
....
....
....
....

What I'm working at now to achieve these goals?

....
....
....
....
....
....
....

Special Notes

My Self-Care Vision Statement

Date: _____ / _____ / _____

Considering my goal and what I would like my self-care to look like in the long term, this is my vision statement...

My Self-Care Goals

Date: _____ / _____ / _____

30 Day Self-Care Goals

....
....
....
....
....
....
....
....

10 Day Self-Care Goals

....
....
....
....
....
....
....
....

Long Term Self-Care Goals

....
....
....
....
....
....
....
....

What I'm working at now to achieve these goals?

....
....
....
....
....
....
....
....

Special Notes

My Self-Care Vision Statement

Date: _____ / _____ / _____

Considering my goal and what I would like my self-care to look like in the long term, this is my vision statement...

My Self-Care Goals

Date: _____ / _____ / _____

30 Day Self-Care Goals

....
....
....
....
....
....
....

10 Day Self-Care Goals

....
....
....
....
....
....
....

Long Term Self-Care Goals

....
....
....
....
....
....
....

What I'm working at now to achieve these goals?

....
....
....
....
....
....
....

Special Notes

My Self-Care Vision Statement

Date: _____ / _____ / _____

Considering my goal and what I would like my self-care to look like in the long term, this is my vision statement...

My Self-Care Goals

Date: _____ / _____ / _____

30 Day Self-Care Goals

10 Day Self-Care Goals

Long Term Self-Care Goals

What I'm working at now to achieve these goals?

Special Notes

My Self-Care Vision Statement

Date: _____ / _____ / _____

Considering my goal and what I would like my self-care to look like in the long term, this is my vision statement...

My Self-Care Goals

Date: _____ / _____ / _____

30 Day Self-Care Goals

....
....
....
....
....
....
....

10 Day Self-Care Goals

....
....
....
....
....
....
....

Long Term Self-Care Goals

....
....
....
....
....
....
....

What I'm working at now to achieve these goals?

....
....
....
....
....
....
....

Special Notes

My Self-Care Vision Statement

Date: _____ / _____ / _____

Considering my goal and what I would like my self-care to look like in the long term, this is my vision statement...

My Self-Care Goals

Date: _____ / _____ / _____

30 Day Self-Care Goals

....
....
....
....
....
....
....

10 Day Self-Care Goals

....
....
....
....
....
....
....

Long Term Self-Care Goals

....
....
....
....
....
....
....

What I'm working at now to achieve these goals?

....
....
....
....
....
....
....

Special Notes

My Self-Care Vision Statement

Date: _____ / _____ / _____

Considering my goal and what I would like my self-care to look like in the long term, this is my vision statement...

My Self-Care Goals

Date: _____ / _____ / _____

30 Day Self-Care Goals

10 Day Self-Care Goals

Long Term Self-Care Goals

What I'm working at now to achieve these goals?

Special Notes

My Self-Care Vision Statement

Date: _____ / _____ / _____

Considering my goal and what I would like my self-care to look like in the long term, this is my vision statement...

My Self-Care Goals

Date: _____ / _____ / _____

30 Day Self-Care Goals

....
....
....
....
....
....
....

10 Day Self-Care Goals

....
....
....
....
....
....
....

Long Term Self-Care Goals

....
....
....
....
....
....
....

What I'm working at now to achieve these goals?

....
....
....
....
....
....
....

Special Notes

My Self-Care Vision Statement

Date: _____ / _____ / _____

Considering my goal and what I would like my self-care to look like in the long term, this is my vision statement...

My Self-Care Goals

Date: _____ / _____ / _____

30 Day Self-Care Goals

....
....
....
....
....
....
....

10 Day Self-Care Goals

....
....
....
....
....
....
....

Long Term Self-Care Goals

....
....
....
....
....
....
....

What I'm working at now to achieve these goals?

....
....
....
....
....
....
....

Special Notes

My Self-Care Vision Statement

Date: _____ / _____ / _____

Considering my goal and what I would like my self-care to look like in the long term, this is my vision statement...

My Self-Care Goals

Date: _____ / _____ / _____

30 Day Self-Care Goals

10 Day Self-Care Goals

Long Term Self-Care Goals

What I'm working at now to achieve these goals?

Special Notes

My Self-Care Vision Statement

Date: _____ / _____ / _____

_Considering my goal and what I would like my self-care to look like in the long term, this is my vision statement...

My Self-Care Goals

Date: _____ / _____ / _____

30 Day Self-Care Goals

....
....
....
....
....
....
....

10 Day Self-Care Goals

....
....
....
....
....
....
....

Long Term Self-Care Goals

....
....
....
....
....
....
....

What I'm working at now to achieve these goals?

....
....
....
....
....
....
....

Special Notes

My Self-Care Vision Statement

Date: _____ / _____ / _____

Considering my goal and what I would like my self-care to look like in the long term, this is my vision statement...

My Self-Care Goals

Date: _____ / _____ / _____

30 Day Self-Care Goals

....
....
....
....
....
....
....

10 Day Self-Care Goals

....
....
....
....
....
....
....

Long Term Self-Care Goals

....
....
....
....
....
....
....

What I'm working at now to achieve these goals?

....
....
....
....
....
....
....

Special Notes

My Self-Care Vision Statement

Date: _____ / _____ / _____

Considering my goal and what I would like my self-care to look like in the long term, this is my vision statement...

My Self-Care Goals

Date: _____ / _____ / _____

30 Day Self-Care Goals

....
....
....
....
....
....
....

10 Day Self-Care Goals

....
....
....
....
....
....
....

Long Term Self-Care Goals

....
....
....
....
....
....
....

What I'm working at now to achieve these goals?

....
....
....
....
....
....
....

Special Notes

My Self-Care Vision Statement

Date: _____ / _____ / _____

Considering my goal and what I would like my self-care to look like in the long term, this is my vision statement...

My Self-Care Goals

Date: _____ / _____ / _____

30 Day Self-Care Goals

....
....
....
....
....
....
....

10 Day Self-Care Goals

....
....
....
....
....
....
....

Long Term Self-Care Goals

....
....
....
....
....
....
....

What I'm working at now to achieve these goals?

....
....
....
....
....
....
....

Special Notes

My Self-Care Vision Statement

Date: _____ / _____ / _____

Considering my goal and what I would like my self-care to look like in the long term, this is my vision statement…

My Self-Care Goals

Date: _____ / _____ / _____

30 Day Self-Care Goals

....
....
....
....
....
....
....

10 Day Self-Care Goals

....
....
....
....
....
....
....

Long Term Self-Care Goals

....
....
....
....
....
....
....

What I'm working at now to achieve these goals?

....
....
....
....
....
....
....

Special Notes

My Self-Care Vision Statement

Date: _____ / _____ / _____

Considering my goal and what I would like my self-care to look like in the long term, this is my vision statement...

My Self-Care Goals

Date: _____ / _____ / _____

30 Day Self-Care Goals

10 Day Self-Care Goals

Long Term Self-Care Goals

What I'm working at now to achieve these goals?

Special Notes

My Self-Care Vision Statement

Date: _____ / _____ / _____

_Considering my goal and what I would like my self-care to look like in the long term, this is my vision statement...

My Self-Care Goals

Date: _____ / _____ / _____

30 Day Self-Care Goals

....
....
....
....
....
....
....

10 Day Self-Care Goals

....
....
....
....
....
....
....

Long Term Self-Care Goals

....
....
....
....
....
....
....

What I'm working at now to achieve these goals?

....
....
....
....
....
....
....

Special Notes

My Self-Care Vision Statement

Date: _____ / _____ / _____

Considering my goal and what I would like my self-care to look like in the long term, this is my vision statement...

My Self-Care Goals

Date: _____ / _____ / _____

30 Day Self-Care Goals

10 Day Self-Care Goals

Long Term Self-Care Goals

What I'm working at now to achieve these goals?

Special Notes

My Self-Care Vision Statement

Date: _____ / _____ / _____

_Considering my goal and what I would like my self-care to look like in the long term, this is my vision statement…

My Self-Care Goals

Date: _____ / _____ / _____

30 Day Self-Care Goals

10 Day Self-Care Goals

Long Term Self-Care Goals

What I'm working at now to achieve these goals?

Special Notes

My Self-Care Vision Statement

Date: _____ / _____ / _____

Considering my goal and what I would like my self-care to look like in the long term, this is my vision statement...

My Self-Care Goals

Date: _____ / _____ / _____

30 Day Self-Care Goals

....
....
....
....
....
....
....

10 Day Self-Care Goals

....
....
....
....
....
....
....

Long Term Self-Care Goals

....
....
....
....
....
....
....

What I'm working at now to achieve these goals?

....
....
....
....
....
....
....

Special Notes

My Self-Care Vision Statement

Date: _____ / _____ / _____

Considering my goal and what I would like my self-care to look like in the long term, this is my vision statement...

My Self-Care Goals

Date: _____ / _____ / _____

30 Day Self-Care Goals

....
....
....
....
....
....
....

10 Day Self-Care Goals

....
....
....
....
....
....
....

Long Term Self-Care Goals

....
....
....
....
....
....
....

What I'm working at now to achieve these goals?

....
....
....
....
....
....
....

Special Notes

My Self-Care Vision Statement

Date: _____ / _____ / _____

Considering my goal and what I would like my self-care to look like in the long term, this is my vision statement...

My Self-Care Goals

Date: _____ / _____ / _____

30 Day Self-Care Goals

....
....
....
....
....
....
....

10 Day Self-Care Goals

....
....
....
....
....
....
....

Long Term Self-Care Goals

....
....
....
....
....
....
....

What I'm working at now to achieve these goals?

....
....
....
....
....
....
....

Special Notes

My Self-Care Vision Statement

Date: _____ / _____ / _____

Considering my goal and what I would like my self-care to look like in the long term, this is my vision statement...

My Self-Care Goals

Date: _____ / _____ / _____

30 Day Self-Care Goals

....
....
....
....
....
....
....

10 Day Self-Care Goals

....
....
....
....
....
....
....

Long Term Self-Care Goals

....
....
....
....
....
....
....

What I'm working at now to achieve these goals?

....
....
....
....
....
....
....

Special Notes

My Self-Care Vision Statement

Date: _____ / _____ / _____

Considering my goal and what I would like my self-care to look like in the long term, this is my vision statement...

My Self-Care Goals

Date: .... / .... / ....

30 Day Self-Care Goals

....
....
....
....
....
....
....

10 Day Self-Care Goals

....
....
....
....
....
....
....

Long Term Self-Care Goals

....
....
....
....
....
....
....
....

What I'm working at now to achieve these goals?

....
....
....
....
....
....
....
....

Special Notes

My Self-Care Vision Statement

Date: _____ / _____ / _____

Considering my goal and what I would like my self-care to look like in the long term, this is my vision statement...

My Self-Care Goals

Date: _____ / _____ / _____

30 Day Self-Care Goals

....
....
....
....
....
....
....

10 Day Self-Care Goals

....
....
....
....
....
....
....

Long Term Self-Care Goals

....
....
....
....
....
....
....

What I'm working at now to achieve these goals?

....
....
....
....
....
....
....

Special Notes

Put yourself at the top of your to-do list every single day and the rest will fall into place.

Made in United States
Orlando, FL
15 February 2025